What's Inside?
Trains

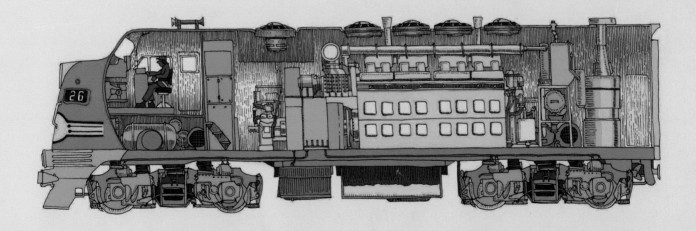

A+
Smart Apple Media

Published by Smart Apple Media, an imprint of Black Rabbit Books
P.O. Box 3263, Mankato, Minnesota 56002
www.blackrabbitbooks.com

Produced by David West ⚇ Children's Books
6 Princeton Court, 55 Felsham Road, London SW15 1AZ

Designed and illustrated by David West

Cataloging-in-Publication data is on file with the Library of Congress.
ISBN 978-1-62588-402-2
eBook ISBN 978-1-62588-436-7

Printed in China
CPSIA compliance information: DWCB16CP
010116

9 8 7 6 5 4 3 2 1

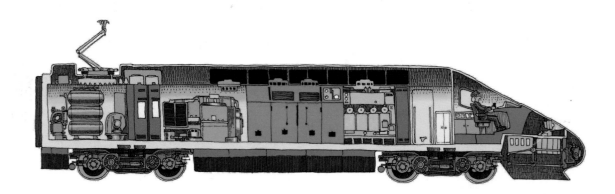

Contents

The first trains were built in the 1800s. They used steam for power.

Steam Locomotive

Wheels

Diesel Electric Trains

Newer trains use diesel fuel. They also use electric power.

F7 Diesel Electric

Engineer

Locomotive

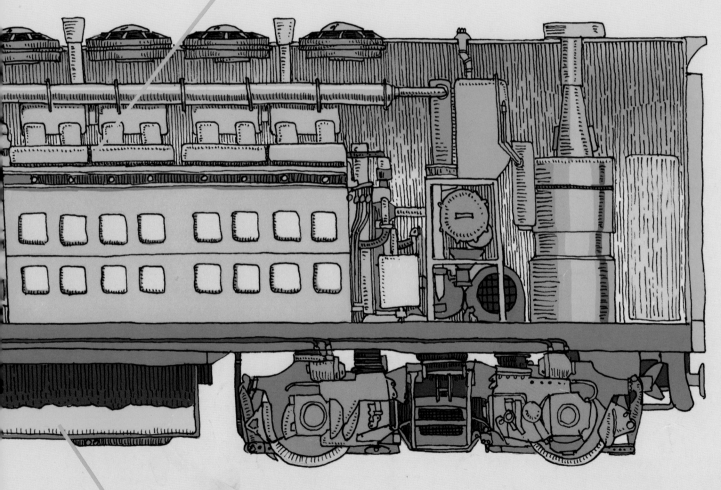

Diesel Engine

Fuel Tank

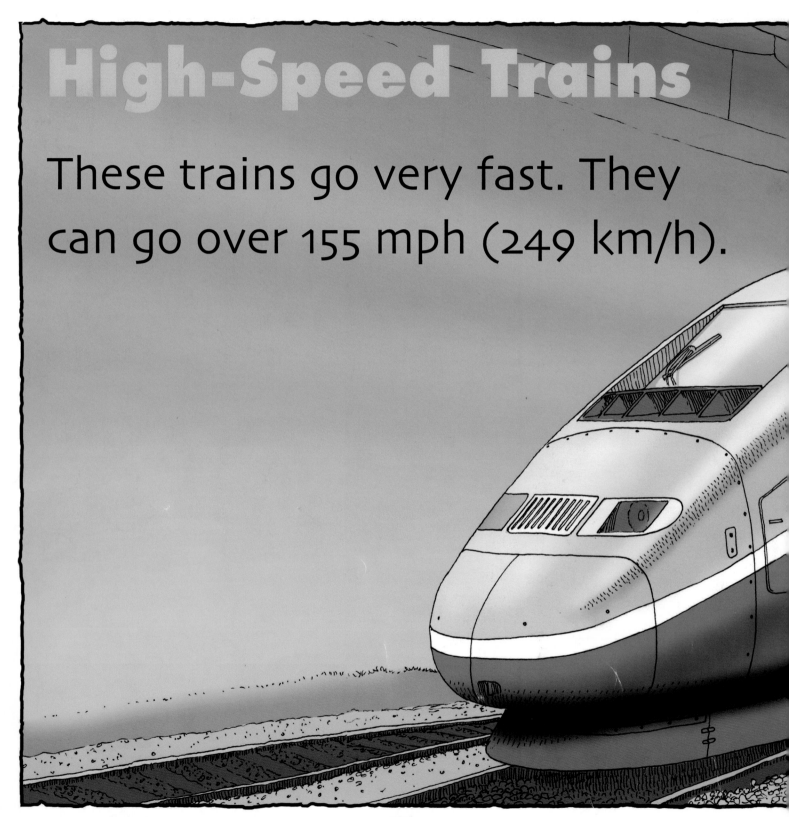

High-Speed Trains

These trains go very fast. They can go over 155 mph (249 km/h).

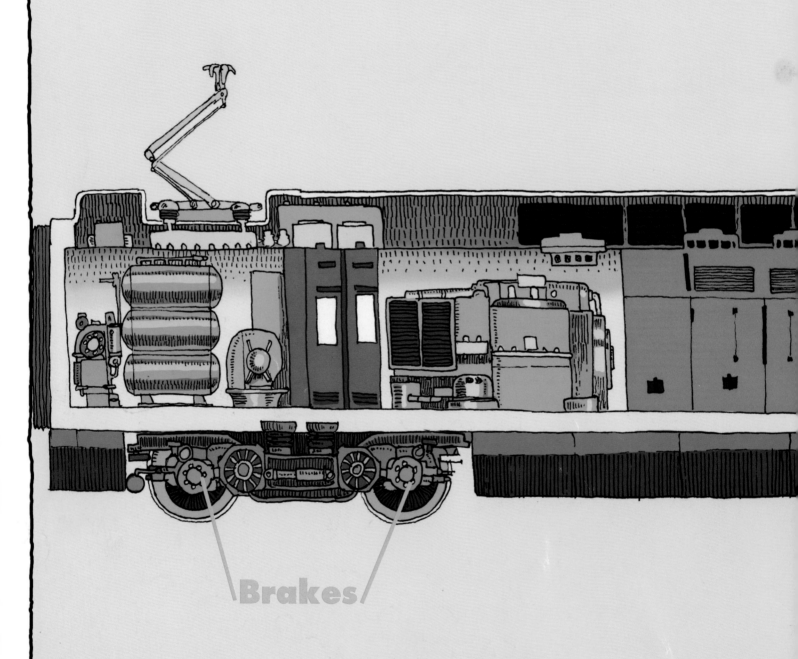

High-Speed Electric

Brakes

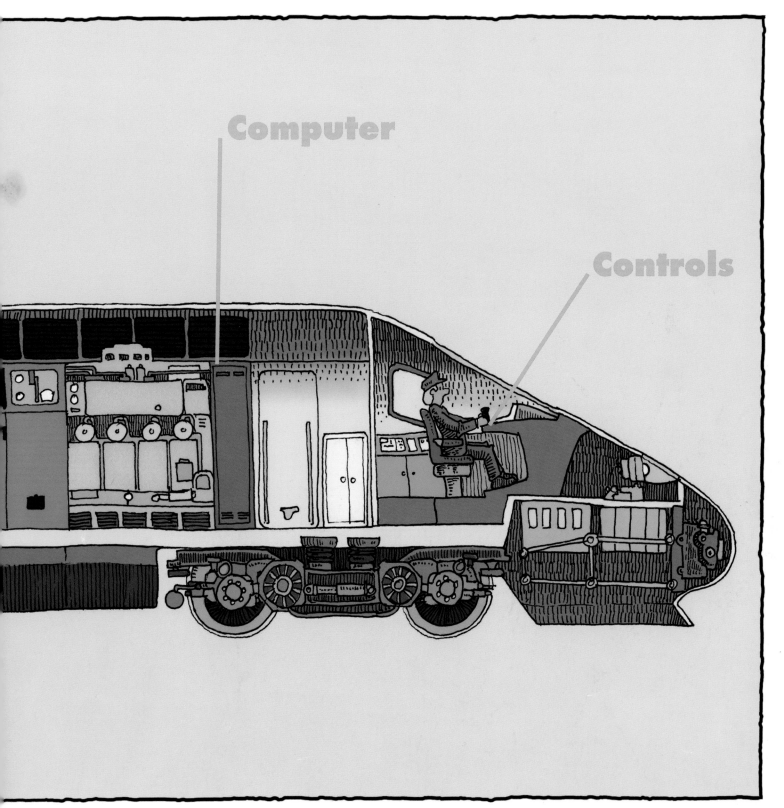

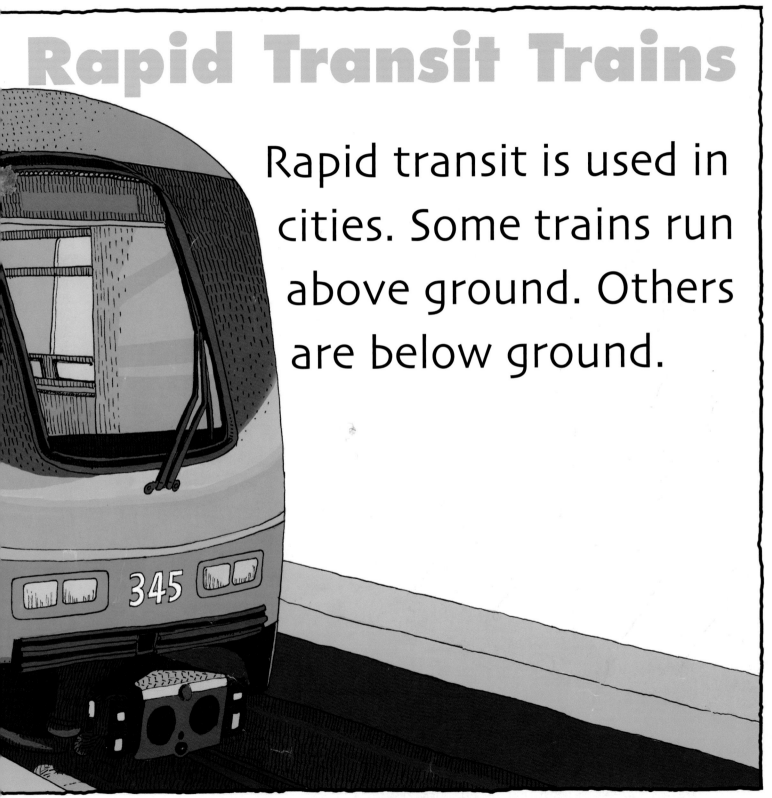

Rapid Transit Trains

Rapid transit is used in cities. Some trains run above ground. Others are below ground.

Urban Metro Train

Brakes

Monorail Trains

These trains run on a large track. They use rubber wheels.

Monorail

Wheel

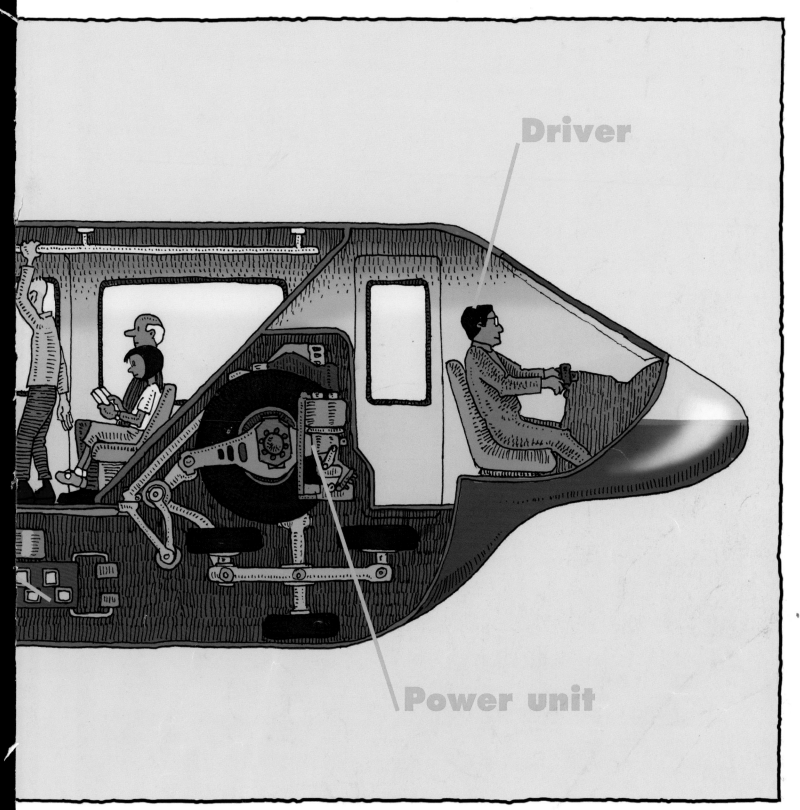

Glossary

boiler

Large container used to heat water to create steam

brakes

Device used to slow or stop a vehicle

diesel engine

Motor that uses diesel fuel to create power

power unit

Device used to move a vehicle

Index